Love
Wisdom

Love Wisdom

Hold a Question in Your Mind
and Wherever You Open This
Book, There Will Be Your Answer

Carolyn Temsi
& Caro Handley

POCKET BOOKS

New York • London • Toronto • Sydney • Singapore

POCKET BOOKS, a division of Simon & Schuster Inc.
1230 Avenue of the Americas, New York, NY 10020

Copyright © 1999 by Carolyn Temsi and Caro Handley

Published by arrangement with Hodder and Stoughton Ltd.
First published in Great Britain in 1999

Library of Congress Cataloging-in-Publication Data

Temsi, Carolyn.
    Love wisdom : hold a question in your mind and wherever you open
this book, there will be your answer / Carolyn Temsi and Caro Handley.
        p.   cm.
    ISBN 0-671-03647-5
    1. Man-woman relationships Handbooks, manuals, etc. 2. Love Handbooks,
manuals, etc. 3. Marriage Handbooks, manuals, etc. 4. Interpersonal relations
Handbooks, manuals, etc. I. Handley, Caro. II. Title.
HQ801.T35 1999
306.7—dc21   99-40380

First Pocket Books trade paperback printing November 1999

10 9 8 7 6 5 4 3 2 1

POCKET and colophon are registered trademarks of
Simon & Schuster Inc.

Printed in the U.S.A.

QF/✕

For Nabil and Jim.
The loves of our lives.
Together we've made our dreams come true.
We love you for your courage, commitment,
integrity and wisdom.
Thank you.

Carolyn and Caro

Our Story

We're best friends who met when we were both hardworking single moms. Carolyn was a marketing consultant running her own business and Caro was a journalist writing for women's magazines. We met through a mutual interest in humanistic psychotherapy and found that we had a lot in common. Both of us were combining our work with bringing up a young child alone, after a history of painful and unsuccessful relationships.

Together we made a commitment to ourselves and each other to find satisfying and successful relationships. We promised that we wouldn't give up until we'd found what we hoped for, no matter how long it took or how hard it got.

The journey meant we had to let go of the ways we'd always done things and learn to do them differently. We had to face uncomfortable truths, most importantly that the only thing standing in the way of our dream was us. We had to be brave, face our fears, learn from our mistakes, deal with obstacles and raise our hopes, our standards and our self-esteem. Which meant recognizing that ultimately we had the power to shape our lives and to choose our futures.

At times it was really tough. We wept, we argued, we took three steps forward and two steps back. Sometimes we came up against something so painful or difficult that all there was to do was cry, laugh, pick ourselves up, dust ourselves off and start all over again, taking with us everything we'd learned from the experience.

And eventually our commitment and our hard work paid off as, one after the other, we found the relationships we wanted. Now we both have love, commitment, respect, warmth, nurturing, laughter, interesting conversation, friendship and honesty. Sometimes it's still tough. But we're dealing with the tough times together with our partners, in loving and supportive relationships. *Love Wisdom* is the result of everything we learned and we've written it for ourselves, our partners, our children and for you.

Introduction

We believe that we all deserve an honest, loving, sensual, sexual, committed, monogamous, respectful relationship.

We believe that this is your right.

Love Wisdom is here to guide and advise you, whether you're in a relationship or looking for one.

Whether you're single, with the person you believe is right for you or looking for the courage to face your difficulties, *Love Wisdom* will answer your questions and set you on the path toward a truly rich and satisfying love.

We have used the wisdom in this book to find love in our own lives. We want to share this wisdom with as many people as possible, so that you too may experience the joy and fulfillment that you deserve.

We wish you well.

How to Use This Book

Here is some guidance on how to form your question:

Keep it simple
Ask for guidance and advice about your question
  rather than yes/no answers
Ask only what you are willing to have answered

If you want *Love Wisdom* to help you, it means:

Treating it with care and respect
Taking your time rather than rushing
Being willing to accept the advice offered
Opening yourself up to the possibility of change
Actively engaging in whatever it requires of you
Accepting the answers, whatever they may be

If you want a more detailed answer, open the book three times while thinking of your question.

The first page will refer to the present moment,
the second to the immediate future
and the third to the long-term future.

Love
Wisdom

Nurture

When you open this book here, it is a time to put the focus onto yourself and your relationship in a gentle and supportive manner. It's time to withdraw from the challenges and demands of the outside world and attend to yourself. Nurture is a call for loving behavior and kindness. Have you been overdoing it? What have you been prioritizing ahead of yourself, your partner, or your relationship? If you are single it is time to nurture yourself before embarking upon a relationship.

It isn't always easy to nurture ourselves as well as nurturing others. Too often in this life we have to put our needs aside and focus on something or someone else. The world is a demanding place. Failing to nurture ourselves and each other can become a habit. It's time to stop and put the focus back on yourself.

You need to nurture yourself now, not tomorrow or next week, but now.

Nurturing means looking after yourself properly. Eating well, getting enough sleep and calming down, away from the stresses and strains of life. Be kind to yourself and to each other. Have a warm bath, bathe your eyes, get someone to massage your shoulders or massage your own, listen to some happy music and think happy thoughts. You already know what feeds your soul; you've just drifted too far away from it. What do you spend the most time doing when you fall in love? Give some of this to yourself now. Love yourself now. Relax. Slow down. Spend time in open spaces. Write a love letter to yourself, buy a gift, leave a note under your pillow. Invest in your heart. The most important element in nurturing is goodwill and compassion. Adopt this attitude and it will quickly become genuine. Nurturing requires a bit of time and effort but a little bit of both goes a really long way.

It's worth it because you're worth it.

Like a flower your relationships will flourish. Start now.

Criticism

When you open this book here, there is negativity around, whether you are aware of it or not. Criticism arises when what we experience doesn't match up with what we want or expect. When we're critical it means we are judging others and finding them lacking. Who are you criticizing? Is it your partner, a potential partner or yourself? Are your standards fair? How would it feel to soften and accept that everyone has their strengths and weaknesses?

The important thing to realize is that criticism feeds on itself and creates a negative spiral. When we feel critical we have locked ourselves into an isolated position where we make the other person our enemy. They don't do or say what we want them to. They look wrong, act wrong, are wrong. We become the blamer. By making the other person totally in the wrong there's nowhere to go to make things better.

If you judge someone's behavior as inappropriate or not fitting with your own values you can deal with this without being critical. Accept it, confront it, talk about it, own it but don't just criticize or attack.

When we get to a critical place in our relationships or with ourselves or potential partners, we need to recognize that it causes more harm than good. Love works best when we're on the same side. If either of you wins, the relationship loses, so take some time out to look at what's going on underneath.

Behind every criticism there's a need. What do you need right now? What would you ask for if you weren't so busy being tough on someone else? Ask and you will receive, as long as you do it without judging the giver. Start looking after yourself more carefully and take responsibility for your resentments at a much earlier stage. If you really are being treated badly stop criticizing and do something about it now.

Life and love are a lot more fun than you're letting them be, so now is the time to make changes.

Trust

When you open this book here, you need to have faith in this relationship or the potential for a relationship. Trust that the future will be well. That any difficulties will be resolved and that your dreams will be realized.

We all create our own realities with our beliefs and expectations. This is telling you that you can have what you want if you trust that you can.

This brings our attention to the importance of trust between two people in order for them to have a successful relationship together. You need to be able to trust each other and both of you need to behave in a manner which is worthy of this trust. Make sure you are absolutely clear what you are trusting each other about and then offer the gift of trust and trustworthy behavior to each other. If your trust has been damaged in the past, deal with your feelings about this now. You can learn to trust again. Base your trust on your true experience. Do not trust blindly, find someone worthy of you to redevelop this part of your nature. Start by developing trust in yourself. Be who you say you are. Be consistent and honest, reliable and true.

If you are struggling with anything right now then trust that you will soon see the benefits of your struggle. Remember that spring always follows winter. Out of struggle comes new growth.

What you focus on grows. Put all of your energies into envisaging the outcome that you desire, while trusting that the results will materialize. Don't try to manipulate, this is about trust, not effort. We don't always get the outcome we want or expect, but what we do get always shows itself to be for the best in the long run. Organize yourself now to be ready, for that which you are trusting will occur. Don't wait for it to happen before you prepare. What we anticipate is drawn to us, and trusting that we will get what we want is part of this process. See it as already accomplished. When you order food in a restaurant you don't go in the kitchen to check if it will be cooked. You trust it will arrive at your table and it does.

Assume your dreams are already in the cosmic kitchen and be ready for when they appear, as they surely will.

Negotiation

When you open this book here, it is time to look at the importance of negotiation in your love life. Negotiation is about finding an agreement which is equally acceptable to all parties concerned. Perhaps you feel that your wants and needs don't matter compared to those of other people. Or perhaps you feel that you should always come first and get what you want. Yet to succeed in love you need to recognize that you and your partner or potential partner both matter equally.

Negotiation is vital to living with and loving another person. You can only negotiate if you believe that you are each entitled to a solution which satisfies both of you. Are you going without or settling for what you don't want, rather than sticking up for your right to be consulted and respected? Do you always get exactly what you want because your partner doesn't stand up for his or her rights? If things go all your way or all theirs, then the relationship is out of balance and in the long run no one can be truly happy. Failing to negotiate leads to bitterness and resentment. If you are stubbornly refusing to negotiate when you could do so without disrespecting yourself, you need to realize that you may win but your relationship will lose. You need to have goodwill in order to create a loving partnership.

Are you finding it hard to negotiate right now? Do you feel that you will be giving in, that you will be giving away all your power? Check that the subject is one on which negotiation is appropriate. Some things are nonnegotiable. If your relationship is monogamous it's not going to work if your partner wants to negotiate about seeing someone else too. You need to get clear about what is up for negotiation and what isn't.

Everyone's wishes, hopes and needs matter. Accept this and you will be able to negotiate with generosity toward others and without compromising yourself. Negotiation is about reaching a position of agreement that you can both accept with goodwill. In negotiating we face our responsibilities to others and their right to be heard as well as our own.

Negotiation is an exciting, challenging skill which enriches and balances our lives.

Giving

When you open this book here, it reminds you that there is a time to give and a time to receive. Now is your time to give. You need to work out what it is that you can give and to whom, as well as the manner of giving which is appropriate. Always give for the sake of giving, rather than because you hope to see it returned.

Some of us are selfish and ungenerous and we need to alter this behavior if our relationships or potential relationships are to flourish. When we fail to give, we keep ourselves closed and we block the flow of energy which is necessary for a healthy relationship. When we live from a belief which says we don't have enough to share, then our lives quickly reflect this belief and it becomes true. The only way to change this is with a leap of faith. When you start to give, more will come to you. You will find more returned to you than you ever gave away, as long as you stay open and don't return to tight, ungiving attitudes and behavior.

There is enough for everyone. We live in a time of abundance. It's only our fear which closes us off from this abundance. Trust that you have enough to share and the reward will be tremendous.

It may also be necessary to take less from your partner right now, while you focus on giving. Encourage them to give less to you so that they can have the pleasure of receiving from you. It's time to shift the balance.

Look carefully at what it is that you actually give and review whether what you give is really what is required. Are you giving money to someone who needs your time or attention, or vice versa?

Are you generous with what you value, as well as with what you don't? Are you giving someone what you want rather than what they would like for themselves? Ask another what they really want from you and see if you're willing to give them what it is that they are asking for.

Give from the heart rather than from the ego to discover the true joy of giving.

Balance

When you open this book here, you focus on the secret of a happy life, as well as on the secret of a healthy relationship. Life naturally finds its own level and if we swing too far in one direction it will always find a way to swing us back as far in the opposite direction, in order to achieve balance.

Right now things are either out of balance in your love life or you are resisting the rebalancing that life is imposing upon you. You need to realize that you can't change the rules on this one. It is impossible to outmaneuver the laws of nature. It's time to remember the old adage "moderation in all things," for this is where we find implicit balance.

What have you been overdoing recently? What are you striving for to the exclusion of its opposite? It's about to catch up with you, unless you make a conscious effort to rebalance things. Are you working or playing too hard? Are you focusing on something else to the detriment of your relationship or potential relationship, or vice versa? Maybe you've developed a mindset that will accept one side of things but rejects its opposite. You want the good in your relationship but don't realize that it comes in a package with what you see as the bad. It's not bad, it's just life balancing out.

What you need to realize is that life is about duality. Everything exists hand in hand with its opposite. Where there is happiness you will also find unhappiness. Where there is generosity there is always selfishness somewhere about. The key is in understanding that this is OK. This is the law of nature. For something to exist, its opposite must also be present. When we accept this, we need only experience the opposite in moderation. But when we pursue one side of something and do everything to avoid its opposite, it comes back at us in an exaggerated form, equal to the size of our rejection of it. The lesson is that it's easier in the end to accept both sides of life and let things balance out along the way. Embrace a bit of negativity and life will send along the good to balance that out too!

Self-Esteem

This is primarily about you because the way you feel about yourself impacts on your relationships. Self-esteem is the sense of worth that you give yourself, the value that you put upon yourself. What's going on right now? Have you been focusing too much on others and so lost touch with yourself? Are you too busy to pay attention to yourself or are you feeling and acting in a critical manner toward yourself? No excuse makes it OK.

To make a relationship work we have to bring two whole people together, rather than try to make a whole from two halves. And you can only be whole when your self-esteem is high. If your self-esteem is low then you will look to your partner to make you feel OK, and this never works. Who are you and how much do you like yourself? Maybe you've let your self-esteem drift. You know you're a good person and you value yourself, but you've just lost touch with it.

Or perhaps this is a more serious warning that you have a real problem with your self-esteem. Maybe this is something you're well aware of but maybe you're not. Ironically, the more strongly you want to argue that this isn't you, the more likely this is to be talking directly to you. So many of us have developed an assertive, confident manner to hide the scared, insecure, vulnerable part inside of us. Real self-esteem is making friends with this part and nurturing it carefully, rather than rejecting it and hiding it away.

When you open this book here it is time to turn inward and get to know yourself more deeply. If you don't keep a journal or diary try writing to yourself every day for a few weeks and see what you find out. Try treating yourself as generously and supportively as you would a best friend and see how much better it feels.

It may be that something is going on in your life that is damaging your self-esteem. Are your relationships exclusive and monogamous? Settling for anything less than this will always bring you pain. Are you being undermined or criticized? Do you feel lovable? Do you pretend to be someone you think others want you to be? Do you let others treat you badly? You will always be treated by others with the level of respect that you give to yourself.

Focus on the fact that you are special and unique. When you love yourself the rest comes easily.

Communication

When you open this book here, your relationship or potential relationship requires clear, honest, direct communication. It sounds so simple yet it is often the biggest challenge that we face.

If the two of you are literally not speaking, the message is clear: you need to open an honest dialogue and talk to each other. Don't attack or criticize. Rather, focus on what you haven't been saying and which you should have said all along. Talk about your own feelings and experiences and don't tell the other person who to be or what to do.

This may also offer a premonition of an impending letter or phone call. It reassures you that the connection is maintained over time and distance and that you will hear from someone soon.

Remember that you can talk to someone using universal energy no matter how far apart you are. It is only a matter of time before telepathic communication becomes accepted as a reality. The really great thing is that you don't have to believe in it to use it. Try sending a message to a loved one with your mind and you'll be amazed at the response. The best time is when they are sleeping as they'll be more receptive. This is a good way to express our vulnerabilities and our wishes, hopes and dreams.

If you feel that you are already communicating well, this warns you that you are not talking about the real issues or that your style of communication is not working. Often we make the assumption that another shares our world of reference. Surely, we believe, if we know what we mean then they must know too. But it may not be the case. Try going back to basics. Ask your partner to tell you what they think you've said and keep repeating it until their understanding is consistent with yours. Then you know you're communicating.

Sometimes we waste huge amounts of time and energy tangled up in communication which is actually designed to avoid the real issue. Now is the time to stop avoiding and to get to the point.

Good communication is at the heart of good relationships. Reap the benefits.

Fun

You have opened this book here to remind you of the importance of fun and playfulness in life. Maybe this is something you've forgotten or lost sight of. Maybe this is a quality that you've never really come to grips with in the first place. Well, now is the time.

The special thing about fun is that it's very personal. What you find fun may well be totally different to someone else, so you need to find out what works for you.

Lighten up and let the laughter flow. Play, enjoy yourself and relax. Bring some energy to having fun. Put a bit of effort in and organize it for yourself. You deserve it.

Often as adults we need to find the humor in life. Even when you feel a long way away from fun, this is what you need. Find the fun in your life in order to bring it into your relationships or to start a new relationship.

What felt like fun when you gave yourself the time to indulge yourself? What makes you laugh? What makes you sing? Let go a little. Live a little. Take some new risks without being irresponsible. Find the child within you. What age are they right now? What's their idea of fun? What would they love you to let them do today? Go to the park, buy some crayons, paints or clay. Tell jokes, throw snowballs, climb a tree, be free.

Without being irresponsible, let the chores pile up and escape for the sheer pleasure of it. Rekindle and reinvent playfulness in your life. If you don't own your fun side any partner will end up exaggerating their fun side and you'll only be jealous. Or they'll drive you mad because too much fun in someone else, when we're not having fun, quickly appears to be selfishness and irresponsibility. Keep the balance by keeping your own fun part alive.

Finally, don't turn having fun into another chore to work hard at. Only do what you really enjoy. Forget the "shoulds"—this is all for you. Remember, having fun is meant to be fun.

Birth

When you open this book here, it signals new beginnings. Birth can be taken literally. Perhaps there is a baby on the way now, or very soon. Perhaps one has just been born. This is about fertility. The time is ripe for new life and new hope.

It can also signify the beginning of a new phase in your relationship, or even a new relationship. If you are hoping to fall in love you can afford to feel very optimistic. Something is gestating and in the near future it will manifest in your life and show itself. Right now you need to make sure that you keep your focus on your dreams and make the most of this period of potential. This is a time to encourage your creativity, to dust off those half-finished projects or start something new. You must admit to yourself what a new beginning would mean to you and then go after it. If you stay true to yourself, anything can be accomplished.

Birth provides you or your relationship with the opportunity of rebirth. You can start again in a new way. A fresh slate is being offered if you are willing to take it. But remember that infancy is the outcome of birth. It's a period of vulnerability and there is a strong need for nurturing and protection. You can't launch a new beginning and then neglect it and hope that all will turn out well. This is a time for focus and gentleness. Get support from those around you; new births don't flourish in solitude. Gather your clan around you and rejoice.

Victim

Occasionally we are innocent victims of other people's mistreatment or manipulation. But mostly, we open the book here to warn us that to play the victim is a choice we make, which secretly suits us. You have given away your power in order to avoid having to take responsibility for yourself and your circumstances.

How are you acting the victim in your relationship? Or are you playing victim by being unable to get into a relationship or keep one going?

It's awful being a victim and the price is huge. No one likes to be around a victim as they feed off other people's energy. When we act as victims we feel powerless while actually holding all of the power. We seem passive but we are putting a lot of effort into staying stuck and seeing things from the wrong perspective. When you are sure that someone else is to blame, when you make excuses or you feel the need to defend yourself, you are being a victim. As a victim we are convinced that there is nothing that we can do and we feel buffeted about by others, fate and circumstance. But it isn't true.

When you refuse to be a victim you instantly create choices for yourself. As a victim, there are none. If there was something you could do about how things are right now, what would it be? What is your part in letting things go on as they are? You always have choices; you only feel like a victim when you forget this. It's time to make a different choice now.

The trouble is that once we get stuck in the victim position, we can only think of passive choices, which rely on other people or circumstances changing. We think that there's nothing we can do. But remember there are alternatives.

You are only powerless in relationships when you give away your power, by relying on another to create the solution. You can't control anyone else, but you can control yourself. Imagine that your circumstances were frozen exactly as they are now and that no one else could ever change them except you. What would you do? You see, you don't have to be a victim once you get active.

You have all the power you need, right now, so use it.

The Wish

This is a good-luck omen. It means that what you wish for is being given extra support at this time and the likelihood is very high that your wish will come to pass.

If you have been waiting for news of some kind, this reassures you that it will be favorable. Your dreams will be realized, so relax and trust that everything will work out.

When wishing we need to be mindful not to try to control someone else or we break the power of the wish. Form your wish in the first person, think in "I" statements to ensure that you wish for yourself. Also leave others out of your wish. For example, if you wish to meet the person of your dreams, don't name them, even if you feel sure of who they are. Maybe your perfect partner isn't known to you but if you are right, it will work out anyway, without you trying to control someone else's destiny.

You need to be very specific about what you wish for. Close your eyes, still your mind and actually picture the result of your wish come true. Make it as real as possible. Where are you? What can you see, touch, smell, hear? When we make our wishes tangible then we help the universal power deliver them to us. We become like a magnet and draw what we envisage to ourselves. The clearer we are the more powerful our magnet. Imagine the wish already well defined, hanging around, waiting to be wanted. The clearer you are, the quicker it will recognize that it is wanted by you and wing its way to you!

When you wish for something be very careful that it is what you really want. It's easy to focus on the positive elements that it will bring into your life, but you have to be sure that you can live with the whole package. Stop for a moment and ask yourself what the drawbacks of your wish could be. If you're honest, there must be some. Now do you want to moderate your wish to take this into account? Remember the saying "Be careful what you wish for, you might just get it." This tells you that you will. So wish with care and with respect for yourself and others and then enjoy!

Resistance

When you open this book here, it is time to look at the ways in which you are resisting the love you deserve. Resistance is the act of working against our conscious intentions, of blocking our own path. Does this sound strange or puzzling? Look carefully at what has been happening in your love life and ask yourself whether or not it could be true. Do you date people who are almost right for you but not quite? Do you talk about how much you want to meet someone and then stay at home and do nothing? Do you tell yourself and others that you are too busy, too old or too independent for romance? Do you keep starting relationships and then get let down? Or do you feel that you know exactly who the perfect partner is but for some reason they're unavailable? What you need to realize is that you avoid relationships, give up too easily or choose unsuitable people as a way of resisting.

If you have been longing for love then you may feel hurt or angry at the idea that a part of you is resisting it. But this is what is happening, and it is only when you accept this part of yourself that you will be able to find lasting love. Embracing your resistance puts the power back in your hands. If it's something that you're doing, then the good news is that it's something you have the power to change.

We only resist for good reason. The part of you which is resisting love is afraid. You may think that you are afraid of being alone and never finding love but the possibility of finding someone who loves and values you is what is really frightening. Letting another human come close enough to find out who you truly are can be very scary. You may be afraid that they can never love the real you, that they will abandon you once they see beneath your outer shell. Or you may be afraid that they will overwhelm, smother or control you. Perhaps you fear re-creating the pain of a previous relationship. The truth is that when we find closeness as adults it stirs up the often forgotten pains of closeness which we experienced as children. We resist romantic love so as to avoid feeling our childhood pain, but then we lose out all over again. You need to let the pain emerge and free yourself to be loved. You can deal with your childhood feelings by recognizing that these are the basis of your resistance and need to be addressed. Now is the time to look inside yourself, find your deepest fears and bring them out. Try going to therapy, try talking to someone about them or write a letter to yourself.

Know that as you face your resistance it will dissolve and leave you free to find the love you deserve. You are brave enough.

Sacrifice

The term *sacrifice* has religious connotations. Traditionally people made a sacrifice of something which they could have taken for themselves, but instead chose to offer to their gods. They did this out of respect, generosity and a faith that they would be protected and provided for. This asks you to apply the same principles to yourself.

This is a time when you need to put someone or something else ahead of your own immediate needs and personal desires. This is a time for sharing and generosity. Now is the time to accept any apparent hardship, or the need to go without, with absolute goodwill. At the same time, you need to trust that in the long term you and your relationships will benefit. Take pleasure in your struggle as an investment in your future. Trust that there will be good reason behind it; this is not about pointless hardship or empty self-denial.

At the same time keep it in perspective. This isn't about sackcloth and ashes. It isn't about being irresponsible and making life as difficult as possible in the hope that the positive return will be equally big. This is about facing the challenge. You need to be willing to put up with things being tough, with good grace, to put yourself out in some way, in your own long-term interest.

The whole notion of sacrifice sounds unpleasant and demanding. Well, this is a demanding time for you, but it doesn't have to be unpleasant. It is all about interpretation. You can define it as you wish.

It is based on the idea of "sacrifice for greater gain." Don't give in or go under if things are difficult right now. You can survive this and more, if you have to. Don't feel powerless. Work out the best way to support yourself and those you love and concentrate on making the best of things. This will pass.

Maybe the real sacrifice is to do exactly what you are avoiding, rather than tolerate things as they are. What extra effort could you make that in the long run would benefit your relationship? Sometimes the sacrifice is to do the thing you're most afraid of. If you're single, maybe the real sacrifice would be to go out there and meet someone, making yourself properly available and open to love. Or maybe it's about holding back and concentrating on yourself first. Be honest about which is really the bigger sacrifice and then be brave and go ahead.

Rescuing

You have opened this book here because you are doing too much for others and not looking after yourself properly. When we are doing or saying something in order to protect others from the consequences of their own actions, we are rescuing. When we feel responsible for the people we care about and we rush in and try to protect them from anything that may cause them distress, we are rescuing. Often we think that rescuing is a good thing, but it is always inappropriate.

Stop and work out how you can untangle yourself from something that isn't yours to resolve. Ask yourself who you are really trying to protect. It's probably you who has the most invested in the outcome, rather than the person whose business it actually is. Did they ask for your help or have you taken over again?

One of the worst aspects of rescuing is that it is so patronizing. It is based on two premises. First, that we know what is best for someone else, and secondly, that they will be unable to cope with their feelings or the result of something if we don't interfere. It's very undermining.

Rescuing is an exhausting process. It leaves us drained and worn-out, as we rush around trying to run someone else's life as well as our own. If you are feeling unappreciated for all of the effort you put into others and feel you don't receive in return, know that you are rescuing and that now is the time to stop!

Mind your own business. It sounds harsh but it's essential, if you want to stop feeling so bitter and put upon. Leave your loved one to get on with things on their own. As adults, they can cope. You may feel guilty. They may try their best to emotionally manipulate you to go back to being responsible for them, but don't be drawn. They'll thank you in the end. Anyone who lets themselves be rescued only ends up feeling controlled, manipulated and angry. They bitterly resent the rescuer while feeling unable to break free and take responsibility for themselves.

Maybe you are hoping that a partner or potential partner will rescue you. Wouldn't it be wonderful if someone would sort it all out for you and protect you from your responsibilities and from being grown up? No it wouldn't. It breeds resentment and discontent. If you want your relationship to flourish, know the difference between support and interference and mind your own business while letting others mind theirs too.

Commitment

This has ultimate importance as an issue. All success in love and relationships rests upon the issue of commitment. Yet it is often the very issue that modern society teaches us least about. A commitment is a pledge, an obligation or a promise. It is something which exists in the present and which also makes a claim on our future.

When you open this book here it's time to go back to basics and remind yourself what commitment is actually all about. The first thing that you need to commit to is the need to have a healthy, loving, supportive, monogamous, long-term relationship. You deserve this and it is your right. Let yourself have it. Don't make excuses. Commit to it and bring it into your life. If you don't know how to do so, go to a good library or bookshop and read about commitment. Talk to others in relationships, go to counseling. Do something to bring it about. When you commit to this and mean it, the rest will follow.

The crunch issue with commitment is that you are making a promise to yourself that you may not want to keep at a later date. For this reason put the bulk of your time and effort into being sure that you mean what you say. Make your word law. Only commit if you really mean it. A commitment is the explicit agreement to a restriction on our freedom or action. Committing to finding a relationship will mean sticking with it through the scary bits too. Yet it is the only guaranteed route to success.

If you are in a relationship and you have opened this book here, check on your commitment. Make sure that it is properly made. Make sure that you are living to it. Remind yourself that real commitment is not about bailing out when the going gets tough. It's about staying and fighting for what is rightfully yours. It will bring you enormous pleasure.

If you or a partner are having difficulty with making a commitment, go easy on yourselves at first. Look at your fears. Deal with the past or any unfinished business. True commitment is a major decision and time is needed to properly judge whether it is appropriate. But make this finite. You don't stand in a shop forever, do you? Shops close, as windows of opportunity close. If you or your partner can't decide, then the appropriate answer is no. Don't stay in a relationship without commitment; it will not work and it will not make you happy.

Remember, commitment and love are a part of each other; always treat them both with respect and you will reap the reward.

Blessing

When you open this book here, it is very special and very positive. There is a blessing for you, your relationship or your potential relationship. The Blessing offers reassurance that relationship issues are being guided by factors outside yourselves. This relationship—or if you're single, your next relationship—is preordained. You two were destined to meet and to experience whatever the qualities and lessons the relationship will provide for you. You have met before and you will meet again, maybe in another lifetime.

You have come together at this time, in this way, for a purpose, whether that is to be soulmates or simply to take a big step along life's path together. Accept that right now, good or bad, things are exactly as they are meant to be. Look for the gift which you are blessed to receive in this relationship. If things are good then rejoice. Appreciate that this is exactly how things should be. Even hard lessons are often very precious gifts. Once you really learn whatever it is this teaches you, you will be free not to have to learn it again.

You can choose where to draw this blessing from, depending on your own personal beliefs, but you need to actively call it into your life. Receive the grace of outside forces. Ask your god, your guardian angel, your fairy godmother or just your good fortune to help, guide and bless this union. You don't need to believe you are blessed to benefit from a blessing, but belief makes it more powerful. Simply ask and it is now yours.

Responsibility

The essence of responsibility is the ability to respond (response-ability) reliably and appropriately. When we judge someone to be responsible it is because they can be relied upon to act in an appropriate and relevant manner at all times. Responsibility contains within it the concept of consistency.

Nowadays we associate responsibility with the mundane tasks of life such as paying the bills and acting in a grown-up manner. It is often dismissed as unappealing, even boring. But true love means being willing to take responsibility. It is the love in our hearts which motivates us to act in a consistently appropriate manner and it is through this that we create the depth and quality of our love.

Now is the time to focus on how we are behaving toward ourselves, our partners or the potential for a relationship. Are you behaving appropriately? Are you treating yourself or your lover in a way that you can be proud of?

Ultimately we need to be responsible for ourselves and our behavior. The antitheses of responsibility are excuses and blame. It is always up to us. We need to respond to our needs for safety, food, shelter, warmth, self-esteem, friendship and good health. We need to respond to our psychological and spiritual needs too. Are you looking after yourself properly? Are you getting the rest and recuperation that you need to be fit to respond to all your other needs? Are you nurturing yourself sufficiently? Are you earning enough money or building up debt? Are you drinking too much or neglecting yourself? What do you need to change in your life to be properly equipped to meet your responsibilities? This will need addressing before a new or current relationship can flourish.

We must also remember that when we enter into a romantic relationship, we take on responsibilities to another as well as to ourselves. Are you taking responsibility for getting your needs met from your partner or are you relying on them to be a mind reader? Are you meeting and respecting their needs appropriately and sufficiently, while encouraging them to be responsible for communicating what these are? Are you keeping to any agreements you have made?

This reminds you that love flourishes when our behavior is consistent with who we say we are and what we say we will do. It calls for a level of maturity which is then rewarded by the quality of love it generates. No excuses, you can do it.

Fantasy

When you open this book here, it is time to look at the role that fantasy is playing in your life. Fantasy is the creation of your imagination. Unlike reality, fantasy is free of restrictions and practicalities. Fantasy can be a wonderful thing, a way of focusing on a dream to help make it a reality, a way of having fun or escaping for a little while. But you are using fantasy in a negative way at the moment—as a way of avoiding full participation in the present and in the reality of your own life. Look at how you are doing this. Do you dream of the perfect partner without doing anything to find them? Do you put up with an unhappy relationship and fantasize about the neighbor or postman to get through each day? If so, you are using fantasy as a way of avoiding the truth, the reality of your life. Now is the time to stop and live in the present. Concentrate on what is real and work on making it better.

Maybe right now you are making something out of nothing in the relationship arena. Stop reading so much into the little that is going on. Stop attributing unknown thoughts and intentions to the person that you are attracted to. If someone looks your way and smiles, that is all that they have done. They haven't communicated a deep desire to be with you. They haven't offered you hope for the future. They simply smiled. If someone doesn't phone you, arrange to be with you, make time to see you and make you a priority, then you are living in a fantasy if you believe that you are having a successful relationship with them. If someone sees you a few hours a week or once every few weeks, the dream of being together is based on hope and imagination, fantasy not reality. Now is the time to face this. Free yourself for someone available and deal with the fears that attract you to someone unavailable. Deal with your fear of real intimacy.

Maybe you opened the book here because your attraction to a movie star or other famous person is filling up your relationship space and blocking the potential for real love. Or, if you're doing this while in a relationship, it's a way of distracting yourself and avoiding full intimacy with your partner. In either case it's time to stop fantasizing and move closer to someone you can really be with.

It's easy to be attracted to famous people or people that we do not know, as they can seem so ideal, but it isn't real. Strip away the glamour and you'll see that these are only ordinary people too. They get grumpy, ill, tired, they go to the bathroom. The fantasy is so perfect because it excludes all of this. It takes you away from real life. But in doing so it robs you of the potential for a true, real and fulfilling relationship. Let go of the fantasy and face reality. Even if it hurts, it's worth it. You're worth someone and something real.

Travel

When you open this book here, the focus is on movement and journeying. It may be that you have a journey already arranged and this assures you of its successful outcome.

If you don't have a journey planned, this may be predicting that you are soon to travel in connection with a relationship. If you are currently single it could be that you are to meet someone special on a future outing. Prepare yourself properly. Travel with optimism and joy. Keep your good humor and embrace any unforeseen interruptions or changes to your journey with a spirit of goodwill and adventure. Be open to your traveling companions but take care of yourself properly and don't expose yourself to risk on a romantic whim. If you are to encounter someone special on a journey it will not require recklessness on your part.

If you have a puzzle or indecision around a journey, know that it will all come clear very soon and that it is vital that you trust your instincts. Close your eyes and ask for the answer to come to you and then trust that it will. You will know what to do when you stop trying to puzzle it out and instead quiet your mind for the answer to make itself heard.

It may be that "travel" is a metaphoric symbol to let you know that right now you are engaged upon a transition in your love life, traveling from one level to another. You may be entering a new relationship or journeying into a different kind of love and commitment. The same rules apply. Look after yourself. Travel is always both exciting and demanding. Try to get a clear idea of where you are headed. But if this proves difficult, then trust that your journey is guided by a force wiser than you, and that your interests will be protected. Soon the destination will become apparent.

Place your attention on the issue of movement within your love life. Whether you are single or involved it is time to stop and think about the direction that you are taking. Are you letting things slide or run away from you? Are you traveling easily or does it feel like pushing water uphill? Are you sailing along happily or maybe getting ahead of yourself with the enthusiasm and desire to arrive at your ideal destination? Look at the issue of movement and direction symbolically in your life.

Remember that traveling is about the experience along the way, not just arriving. Savor the moment a little more; everything is as it should be right now.

Safety

When you open this book here, know that safety is an essential quality for success in love and relationships. Its importance is rarely adequately recognized and as an issue it is frequently misunderstood. The term "safety" means "the freedom from threat of danger or injury" and it includes both your physical and your emotional well-being. You need to stop and review how safe you are feeling at the moment and also the reality of how safe you actually are.

Look first at the obvious issues. Ask yourself some very basic questions. Are you physically safe in your relationship? Is there violence or the threat of violence in your love life? Think carefully when you answer this question. Has violence been escalating in your life recently? Are there doors slammed, glasses broken or any other acts like this which you are trivializing or dismissing? Take these issues seriously, because otherwise they'll only get worse.

If you are looking for a new relationship or have just met someone new this card cautions you to look after yourself properly. Meet in public places and go slowly until you really know that you can trust this person. If they are safe they will respect your caution.

Next, look at your emotional safety. How do you feel in relationships? Do you trust that you can open up and show your true self or are you careful and cautious, always trying to get it right so that you don't leave yourself vulnerable or exposed? In love we ought to feel safe. We deserve to believe that our feelings will be respected. Take this seriously. If something isn't right, it won't go away if you bury your head in the sand.

Or, it may be that you could be safer in your relationship or potential relationship than you realize. Now may be the time to move forward and take the risk of being more open and asking for what you want. Stop and think about what you need to feel safe. You may need to practice this alone before you can share it with another. Find out what it takes to make you feel comfortable. Comfort and safety are intricately linked. When you get better at tuning in to your feelings you'll learn to trust your instincts and you'll know when you are safe and when you're not. Remember, safety is the foundation stone of love.

The Lovers

When you open this book here, it is very special. You can feel happy. The lovers are the essence of what relationships are all about, the two of you exclusively making each other your focus, in order to share the experience of love and relating.

This is about couples. Know that you are being reassured that you have the love that you desire, or that you are soon about to find it. If you are already together, really appreciate what you have, and if you are single, know that the time is coming when this will change.

The Lovers carries with it the condition of exclusivity. It is about two people only. Ensure that there really are only two of you in your relationship or potential relationship. If one of you is getting closer to someone else draw back now, the earlier the better. If you are already close only to each other, then this honors your bond and blesses your union.

The Lovers reminds us of the harmony that exists between two people who are engaged in loving each other. If harmony is lacking, then it reminds us that this is where we need to be placing our energies. Act like a lover, make the extra effort, maintain the mystique. Don't underestimate the importance of your attitude. The power to sustain the Lovers lies in their own hands.

This encourages us to remember what we are seeking through loving. It puts our focus on pleasure and romance. It asks us to indulge our dreams and fantasies. Buy a romantic card, take a risk, be extravagant. Love is allowed to be larger than life and so are you.

The Lovers also reminds us of the importance of sensuality. Make time to enjoy the physical pleasures of love, as a couple or alone. Taste, touch, smell the things that make you happy. Pay due respect to the senses and make time for each other. Don't slip into taking each other for granted. You deserve time for love and time for loving.

However, the Lovers must also respect the foundations of love. Enjoy the pleasures, but do not neglect those aspects which call for effort and consistency. Put work and commitment into the relationship over the long term and combine it with romance and sensuality. Neither should be the icing on the cake. Commitment needs sensuality and sensuality needs commitment. The Lovers need them both. Enjoy.

Bravery

When you open this book here, it is time to be brave. Something is required of you which is not necessarily easy or comfortable. You need to draw on your courage and face it head-on. Avoidance and timidity are not working. The longer you procrastinate, the longer you put off accomplishing your goal.

We all have bravery within us and for each of us it will mean different things. We each have our own Achilles' heel. Some people find it easy to climb mountains and jump out of planes yet they are terrified of spiders. It is the same with our love lives. Some of us are terrified of intimacy in relationships, always making ourselves unavailable or falling for someone we can't have or who never quite fits the bill. Others are comfortable with intimacy yet they are scared of commitment, staying in the relationship but making no promises for the future. Still others are scared of self-responsibility, leaning heavily on a partner for all their needs.

Now is the time for you to admit what your issue is and start dealing with it. It's time to let someone available and suitable come close. It's time to deal with those old buried feelings that keep you so needy or so fiercely self-reliant. Maybe it's time to leave, or time to admit that you're never leaving.

Bravery means making a resolution and following it through. It means not giving up when the going gets tough. It means being willing to try new things and experience the discomfort of stretching ourselves beyond what feels familiar and comfortable. It means going beyond where we've been before and trusting that we will have the resources to succeed and to handle our feelings. Most importantly being brave means being willing to acknowledge that we are scared and to feel this fear without letting it prevent us from doing what we need to do. It's easy to imagine that brave people don't experience the level of fear that we do, but it isn't so. Their bravery lies in being willing to press on through the fear, knowing that it is the only way. Your feelings will follow your behavior, not the other way around. If you wait to stop being scared before you make a move, you will wait forever. Yet, if you do it while feeling the fear, then the fear will begin to recede. The fantasy of how scary something will be is usually worse than the reality but without bravery you will never find this out.

What do you need to be brave about? Who do you need to confront? How do you need to change? What would you do, how would you run your life if there was nothing to be scared of? While respecting others and not breaking the law or endangering your health or safety, you need to start taking some risks in your love life. Go on, be brave. Now is the time.

Separateness

When you open this book here, it is time to recognize the individuality of every person. Each of us is an individual, whether we are deeply caught up in a romantic, committed relationship or we are alone. Separateness is an important quality which we need to monitor and negotiate in order to have successful relationships.

If you are single, you must respect your separateness and protect your identity when approaching a new relationship. This doesn't mean avoiding commitment and prioritizing yourself over someone else's needs. But it does mean holding on to your true identity and values. You don't have to become who you think someone else wants you to be. Be yourself and then you'll end up with the right person, who wants someone just like you.

If you are in a relationship Separateness reminds you that you are both individuals within this romantic unit. Who are you? Do you know? Does your partner know? Sometimes we get so stuck in being nice to each other that we lose track. Other times we get so stuck in conflict or in defending ourselves that there's no space for who we are when we are alone.

All of us need to reflect on our separateness. Enjoy a little space to reconnect with yourself. Practice defining yourself while still respecting others. What is your opinion? Don't look to another to tell you what you think, you already know. What do you like, want, wish for?

The need for separateness can also arise when we don't have enough space between us. Our dependency needs, or theirs, push us toward a partner or prospective partner, so much so that we choke out the light. We want to feel safe and loved but we don't realize that we can still feel secure with enough space for some fresh air to circulate. We can.

It's all about balance, trust and honesty. You really can have a connection and still stand back a little and let the sun shine through. It's safe to be you.

Addiction

This has a rather serious title because it covers a very serious topic. When you open this book here, know that there is addiction somewhere around your relationships.

This may be an obvious physical addiction. Is someone drinking, smoking, eating, taking drugs, gambling in an addictive way? We can't have successful relationships while we ignore our addictions. We need to deal with them. Yet most addictions are insidious. They are so much a part of normal society, which is rife with addiction, that they are surrounded by denial. Who wants to admit that an addiction is really present? We use them to avoid the truth, not to face it.

It is time to face the truth. Even the smallest step in the right direction is a start. One of the benefits of our addictive society is that there is now so much affordable help for addicts. You only have to reach out and you'll find it. Pick up the phone, ask your GP, enquire at the library, or write to a problem page. Help is at hand.

It may be your partner, ex-partner or future partner who has the obvious addiction but there is a clue to your own addictive process in your attraction to them.

Addictions are about trying to avoid our feelings. We feel compelled to do something to distract ourselves from feelings which would be painful, uncomfortable or unfamiliar. Instead we act addictively; anything will do as long as it works to keep us from the feelings we are trying to avoid. We use work, shopping or TV, not just alcohol. Relationships are another socially acceptable form of addiction. When we can't bear to be apart, when we are intoxicated with love it's often hard to see it as addiction. But when this goes on past the honeymoon period, or if things are very volatile, and we can't live together or apart, these are signs that we are using someone else to avoid our feelings.

The good thing is that the feelings which we are trying to avoid are actually bearable. It is the energy collected while avoiding them that makes them feel unbearable. Yet if we start to let them come and accept them, they gradually diminish and we learn that we can survive them. Be brave. Recognize the addiction, inhibit the usual attempt to avoid your feelings and dare to have them. They won't last or overwhelm you even if you're afraid that they will. True love lives on the far side of addiction and the only route there is through your feelings. You can do it.

Childhood Issues

When you open this book here, it means that your childhood is influencing your capacity to have successful relationships.

Our adult relationships are always affected by what we learned and witnessed as children. But sometimes the influence is too great and too negative.

Stop and review the rules around relationships that you picked up as a child. Were your parents together or apart? Did you see love, truth, communication and respect? Or lies, dishonesty, unfairness and disrespect? What have you carried forward into your relationships now? Are you looking to your partner to parent you because you didn't get enough of what you wanted from your own parents? Are you looking for a stand-in, because one or both of your parents were physically or emotionally absent or unavailable in your childhood? Are you very controlling, because this was your role in your family, or do you feel smothered as you did as a child? Look carefully at what is going on.

Review the beliefs or rules which guide your relationships. What do you think is right and wrong? How do you expect to act or be treated? Now find the links between this and your upbringing. Are you making free, informed, adult choices, or are you restricted by the past? Take the time to take stock of whatever remains unresolved from your childhood. This is where the answers lie and this is what needs your attention. It may be that this is your partner's issue too, but don't use this as an excuse not to look at yourself. This is about you.

This can be a warning that you haven't separated appropriately from your parents. Are you free to make your own decisions about who and how you love? If not, it's time to cut the umbilical cord and grow up. It's time to be yourself rather than the child that you once were. You need to leave home emotionally, as well as physically.

It's important not to use your relationships as an act of rebellion. If you always had to be reliable then, you don't have to be untrustworthy now to prove you've grown up. Make your own choices, for yourself, not for anyone else.

It's time to resolve the past and leave it behind. But you won't do that successfully without learning from it and recognizing how it is influencing you.

Appreciation

You opened this book here to remind you that we always have elements that we can appreciate in our lives and in our relationships. This may signify a very happy, satisfying period in your relationship. If you have just found love, give thanks. If you are looking for love, appreciate those that you encounter on this path.

Appreciation calls us to count our blessings. If life is good it is easier to be full of appreciation. Yet it is when times are difficult that appreciation becomes all the more important. What do you have to be thankful for? From the smallest to the largest element of life. Be grateful that you can draw breath, that your heart pumps life around your body, that you are free to think your own thoughts.

Appreciate the love and support in your relationships and if times are difficult, appreciate having someone to struggle and grow with at this time in your life, regardless of what the future brings. Every experience is a lesson. Every day makes us a different person from the one we were yesterday. Appreciate that you have the choice to influence who you are. The present and the future are your own.

One of the fundamental rules of life is that "what you focus on, grows." This is particularly true with appreciation. Think negatively and life gets worse, but give your attention to what is good and you will discover more that is good.

If you're looking for a new relationship, appreciate the ones you have already had. Appreciate yourself and what it is like to be single right now. If you are planning to leave a relationship, appreciate what you have had, all that has been good and that you have the freedom to move on.

Feed yourself and your love life by focusing on what you have to appreciate and watch this grow and grow.

Projection

You open this book here when you are seeing qualities in another which really belong to you. This can be hard to see and sometimes even harder to admit.

We are usually so convinced that whatever the issue is, it is about the other person. It's their anger, their selfishness, their weakness, their passivity. It's they who are boring or difficult, or so it seems. We do this with positive qualities too. We insist that the other person is brave, honest or trustworthy, loving, kind or thoughtful, but so often we are seeing what we project onto them. They are simply the movie screen; it is we who create the movie. Try to see past what you are projecting to find who your partner or potential partner really is. And take responsibility for what you project in order to learn more about yourself.

The value of "projection" is to direct you back to yourself. Whatever the quality you see in another, you need to look for it in yourself, whether it is good or bad. If someone else is angry, know that it is you who are angry even if you are not showing it. If they seem mean or dishonest, focus on the ways in which you are mean and dishonest. When you deal with whatever aspect of yourself you're projecting onto someone else, it will mysteriously diminish in the other person. Then you will be able to see who they really are.

Much of the purpose of relationships is to allow us this screen to project our movie onto. How else would we know what we have on our own film if we didn't have a screen to view it on? But it also creates the bulk of relationship problems. To solve them you have to think of your partner as a mirror which is allowing you to meet yourself. If what you see is a problem, then focus on changing this in yourself, not in them. The more you can unravel this, the more likely it is that you can have a real relationship which goes beyond projection and is more rewarding.

Marriage

When you open this book here, it signifies union. This can be very literal. It can mean a recent or impending marriage, and it can also refer to cohabitation in a relationship. Marriage acknowledges the existence of the unit that the partners create. It can refer to an emotional marriage where the love between you is creating its own deep bond, as well as an actual marriage.

You may have just met, already be with, or be about to meet, your soulmate. Or this may refer to a marriage that doesn't last. It signals that you are with the perfect partner right now for you to work with, to find a deeper understanding of what relationships are all about. Know that if you learn the lesson here, a lasting union will follow.

Remember that marriage is about serious vows. They remind us that union is "for better or worse, for richer or poorer, in sickness and in health." You need to pull together whatever the circumstances, to support each other at all times, not just when it's easy. This is the lesson of Marriage.

Marriage can also indicate a need for you to bring together two parts of yourself, which up until now you have kept very separate. In order to be fully whole we have to integrate all of our aspects and this is directing you to consider taking that step and exploring an internal marriage. Do you live your life in separate compartments? Do you show one side of yourself in romantic relationships and another side to friends or family? This is telling you it's time to be whole, it's time to join with either yourself or another and then to reap the benefits. Marriage brings integration, togetherness and completion.

Repetition

Repetition can be both frustrating and liberating. You need to stop and review what's going on for you with regard to relationships, because here you are again, something is being repeated.

Look for what is uncomfortable yet familiar. Admit that you have been here before. Face the fact that although the people, the details or the circumstances may have changed, you are back in the situation that you've found yourself in before. Whether this is a more extreme version or a less extreme one, look for the similarities rather than the differences. Then you will see what the lesson is that you are meant to learn from these events.

When we deny and justify, blame and make excuses, we miss the purpose of finding ourselves in these exact circumstances. Life is a series of lessons to be lived. When we find and learn the lesson we can move on and let go of the need for the events which teach us the lesson. But when the lesson reappears, in the old or a new form, it means either that we didn't really learn it last time, or that there is still more to be learned. This is your opportunity. If you want to be free from repetition you have to liberate yourself by facing what it is that you're not yet finished with.

Take comfort in the fact that many of us revisit the same lesson over and over again to learn it. Yet, even if we only learn a little every time it reappears in our lives, this will be enough to make the repetition less painful and less traumatic next time.

Don't feel downhearted if you've been making progress yet the lesson has come to you bigger than ever this time. It may be a final clearing. But be warned. If you deny whatever it is, each time it reappears, you won't learn. Then the lesson will only get more painful and more dramatic in an effort to break through your denial.

In the end you'll have to face it. One way or another. Why not do it now, softly, softly?

Financial Issues

When you open this book here, you need to consider the impact of your finances on your relationship. Is lack of money, or even an excess, causing stress between the two of you or preventing you from finding a relationship? Is the relationship balanced financially? Look at who has the power and who is controlling who financially.

The most frequent issue arising here is resentment. People fool themselves that they are comfortable with financial arrangements which bring them satisfaction at a surface level. Maybe it's nice to be the provider or to be provided for. Yet unless you are both in total agreement about this it can undermine the balance of the relationship. If you don't acknowledge this it can fester below the surface. Look at what you get out of continuing with a particular financial arrangement or behavior which disempowers one of you. Get clear around money issues between you and stick to what you agree to. It's an easy place to fudge the truth but it always comes back to haunt us. Money issues are very important—don't ignore them.

This can also be telling us to deal with our own issues around money rather than focusing on our partner's or a potential partner's issues. Are you hoping to find someone rich or trying to buy love? Look at how this is affecting you.

It's always easier to see inappropriate financial behavior in another than in ourselves. But look to yourself, and leave others to their own lessons, unless they're dragging you down with them. If this is the case, deal with it.

The most important truth is that money is simply energy. Waste it and you waste yourself, hold on too tightly and you strangle the life out of it. Look at how your finances reflect the energy flow in your love life and deal with what you find. It won't heal on its own.

Family Pressure

When you open this book here, your relationships are being influenced by other people. These are likely to be relatives and immediate family, but you may also need to look at who you consider to be your family. Who do you spend most of your time with and where does your emotional commitment lie? Maybe they are your family at work, a sports team, or a group of friends.

Family pressure can signify family disapproval and a lack of support for your approach to relationships or potential partners. If you feel you are being supported by your family, look again and question whether the relationship is really being supported. Useful support is not divisive, it does not pit one person against another. It does not judge or criticize. It recognizes that there are two sides to every story and that only those involved in any relationship can ever really know if and how it works.

Are you feeling under pressure to stay loyal to family members who do not support your relationship choices? If so, it may be time to loosen these family ties. Being adult is about creating your own family now. You can choose to surround yourself with people who offer you and your relationships love and support.

Family pressure can also signify pressure from within the family unit or group of people that you live with. Are you and your partner pulling in different directions? Are the kids, or is the desire for kids, driving you mad, wearing you out? Do you need a break or do you need more time together? Is someone in your family expressing problem behavior? Realize that this can be because you and your partner are unwilling to recognize and deal with your own problems, so they are acting these out for you.

Are the two of you in conflict about your commitment to your extended families, or about the issue of being a family yourself? Who are you trying to please? The best action is to bring the focus back to yourself or the two of you. Get clear about your own priorities and what is best for you around any relationship. But do so with respect and goodwill for those outside you. Most importantly, don't agree to compromises you don't really believe in.

Take time to work through whatever the issue is. Get active, attempt to relieve the pressure. Of course, with some family pressures there may be nothing you can do but wait this out. If this is the case, focus on making things as easy as you can for the both of you in the meantime.

Standards

When you open this book here, it is to remind you of the importance of having and keeping realistic standards in your relationships. Standards are the example against which something is measured or judged. You have to know what you think is right in order to judge whether something measures up to it or not. Standards are tied up with morality, integrity, honesty, decency. These are vital qualities for truly satisfying relationships. The backbone of love.

What are your standards when it comes to love? Do you believe in loyalty, respect and commitment? Do you expect monogamy, nurturing and to be prioritized above others? Do you believe that partners should make themselves available for each other on a regular basis or will you settle for playing second fiddle to your partner's other priorities? You need to question what your beliefs are. You need to get clear about whether you have a standard on a certain subject and how to go about developing one if you don't. People with high standards are the most successful in love. Talk to people you respect, who have relationships that work well and then value their advice. And when you've got a decent standard, make sure that you stick to it. Don't just settle for what you can get. Don't compromise yourself and make excuses, because this doesn't work. Now is the time to stop.

When you believe that you are precious and valuable you will expect to be treated as such. When you know what you are worth you set your standards high and you won't settle for anything less. But right now you don't know what you are worth. Although you may have high self-esteem in other areas of your life, you have low self-esteem around love. You are entitled to high-quality loving yet you don't know it. You don't have to settle for crumbs anymore. Doing so keeps you in a vicious circle. The crumbs keep you hungry and then you're grateful for any more crumbs that you can get. You need to realize that when you hold out for a higher standard of love, you will be full enough to recognize crumbs for what they are, just crumbs.

Focus on the basics first. You deserve to be respected. Your partner should phone when they say they will, turn up on time and be interested in you and your life. Then work at expecting and getting much more than this.

You may need to check your own behavior against these standards. Do you treat partners with goodwill and respect? Do you keep your word? We need to live with high standards to be treated well. Remember, the world always reflects our own behavior and attitudes back at us through others. It's easy to criticize others without looking closely at ourselves. Raise your standards, stick to these standards and enjoy the rewards you will reap.

What Goes Around,
Comes Around

This is a vital law of nature, although sometimes we have to look at the bigger picture to see just how true it is. This reminds us that whatever we put out in the world always comes back to us and it does so in an exaggerated form. Even if it isn't apparent to you, know that this always holds true in our relationships.

What Goes Around, Comes Around asks us to treat others as we would wish to be treated. To act with love and goodwill. To be kind, supportive and nurturing. To remember where we begin and end and not meddle in other people's business. To support without taking on another's responsibilities and to not make others responsible for us. To act with honesty if we wish to experience honesty. If we are unkind, dishonest or selfish with our love and goodwill, we will be treated in the same way. If we use people, we will find ourselves being used by others. You need to look carefully at what it is you send around and which is going to come back to you. Are your standards slipping? Have you got caught up in being critical or judgmental? Is this how you want your partner or potential partner to act toward you?

When we feel that we are being treated badly, unkindly, dishonestly or in any other way which causes us pain, this rule is also relevant. You need to recognize that you have created this experience in your life. What you put out earlier has come back to you. You can change it by putting out something different and better. Stop putting out negative qualities and they will no longer return to you in this way. Start now because we create the future in the present. Be generous with what "goes around" from you and enjoy the pleasures of what will then "come around" in the near future.

Transition

When you open this book here, the issue is change. You are in the process of moving from one time to another. One way of being to another. Things are not how they were and neither are they how they will be in the future. This is the period between the two, the transition. It is important to label what is happening when we alter an old structure or way of being, in order to form a new one. It is an exciting and rewarding experience, but it can feel very uncomfortable, scary and even chaotic. Realize that this really is OK.

At a time like this it is important to trust the process. While it may seem that things do not make much sense right now, a new structure is emerging. It is already forming beneath the surface, it just hasn't shown itself yet.

You need to go with whatever is presenting itself most strongly right now rather than resisting it. You can't go backward, even if you want to. The wave has crashed on the shore, it is no longer the perfectly formed structure that it was. Rather, it is a seething mass of froth and white water. Momentarily the order and the clarity are lost but it will reform into a new wave, equally beautiful, equally perfect but different. It is already happening under the surface.

If external events reflect transition, don't be mistaken by thinking that this is all that is happening. Recognize the transition that is less apparent and support any deeper change, in yourself, or between the two of you. Don't try to control everything too tightly. The new wave needs room to form.

Dishonesty

When you open this book here, there is something that is not straight and honest around your relationship. Does your heart sink when you read this? Do you know exactly what this is referring to, although you'd rather ignore or deny it? Well, now is the time to face it. Healthy relationships don't function in conjunction with dishonesty. Honesty is essential. It's crucial for love and happiness, and unless you face this you will never have peace.

If you can't make an obvious link between your life now and the issue of dishonesty, then you need to dig a little deeper because it is there. Dishonesty is one of life's slippery characteristics which we in turn can be dishonest about. "I'm not stealing, I'm just taking something left lying around," "I'm not cheating, I'm just having a night out with another man." This is the way we lie to ourselves, and once we've taken ourselves in, then we lie to those around us. It will end in tears. You always pay for dishonesty and the price is high.

Sometimes, our dishonesty is about not speaking up. We don't declare our thoughts or feelings about something which actually matters. Be brave enough to say what you think. Make sure that your behavior matches your words.

If you think that the dishonesty here refers to your partner, or potential partner, and not to yourself, then you'll actually find that it refers to both of you. If someone isn't being straight with us we often don't want to face it. So we refuse to face it when the facts don't quite fit or our gut has that sinking feeling. We always know a lot more than we admit when someone isn't telling us the truth. If you get honest with yourself then their dishonesty will be exposed.

It takes courage but facing dishonesty brings its own rewards.

Codependence

When you open this book here, know that you are creating your own happiness. Codependence is about putting your partner's or potential partner's needs in front of your own, to a degree where your needs don't get addressed or even admitted. We're all familiar with the line "I'm happy if you're happy," but if that is how you run your life it really won't work. It means that your only power to make yourself happy is to make your partner happy first. Sadly, you never have any guarantees that you can do that. It also means that to accomplish this you'll have to neglect yourself and what you want.

Codependent behavior involves looking after someone else (whether practically, emotionally, or both) with the expectation that once they've got what they want, then there will be room for what you want, or in the hope that they too will be codependent enough to prioritize you ahead of themselves.

Of course, if they've got any sense at all, they won't do this. They'll know that they need to be the priority in their own lives. They can respect your needs and negotiate for mutual happiness but if they're wise, and noncodependent, they won't be untrue to themselves and then think that good will follow. When you're codependent, it's easy to think that this means that you're kind and generous and that someone who isn't is mean and selfish, but it isn't true. Codependence is bad news.

Often people get caught up in mutual codependence, both trying to satisfy each other and hoping that the other will satisfy them next. It gets complicated and messy. Why try to guess what the other wants and then try to provide it for each other, when you can simply be honest about what you want yourself and sort out the best way to get it?

Take your focus off the other person and put it onto yourself. Get clear about what you feel or what you want. Start communicating about this and start looking after yourself. Trying to get what you want while never admitting what it is creates so much resentment and leads to unnecessary, overcomplicated negotiations. Get honest, get selfish in the best sense of the word. Do yourself a favor and define yourself.

Saying who you are, what you feel and what you want can feel very scary. It flies in the face of convention yet it is the only path to happiness and successful relationships. Be true to yourself and everything else will follow. Do it respectfully and do it now.

Meditation

When you open this book here, your life and your relationship are going through a period when you are spending more time alone and feeling more separate than usual. Meditation is directing you to make the most of this space that life is providing for you. Spend time actually thinking about yourself and your relationships. Involve yourself in activities that nurture you and that give you time to really feel connected with yourself and the world around you.

Maybe you need to rest and relax more, to organize "quiet time" where you unhook the phone, turn off the TV, put down what you're reading and actually say "Hello" to yourself. Have a conversation with yourself. Find out what you want to do in this quiet time. Don't put too much pressure on yourself. Maybe you could do five minutes twice a day, rather than making more ambitious plans and then not be able to follow through with them.

True meditation is about quieting our inner voice, creating a peaceful, clear space in which to connect with our own spirituality and inner wisdom. It's in this quiet space that you will learn to hear the voices of the guardian angels who surround and protect you. Try meditating in a way that suits you. Buy a tape or a simple book to teach you the basics. You don't have to follow it exactly. Relax and find out what works for you. One of the simplest and most effective ways to learn meditation is through yoga. It is truly powerful.

By contrast, if your life has very little time or space in it for you, then this is warning you that you need to make changes. You need to take space for yourself or you'll soon see the consequences of this self-neglect. You are important and no one is indispensable every hour of the day. Don't plan it for next week or next month, do it now and both you and your relationship will benefit.

Darkness

When you open this book here, know that times are tough. Maybe your relationships aren't working as well as you had hoped they would. Or perhaps one or both of you may have been through a particularly difficult time. Maybe you're finding it really hard to establish a satisfying relationship. The problem you're now experiencing may be obvious or this may signify a more subtle underlying unhappiness.

Stop and take stock of what you've been going through. Give yourself a cup of tea, a hug and some sympathy. Have you fully acknowledged how tough things have been? Have you talked this through with someone you trust or with your partner? There's a lot of relief and validation in acknowledgment. Mark this difficult time and then be prepared to move on. The good news is that darkness never lasts. Life pulsates. Life is about rhythm. Just as we breathe in and out and as our heart closes and opens as it beats, so good follows bad and new life follows death. The darkest hour is always just before the dawn.

Breathe a sigh of relief. Know that easier times are ahead. Know that this period of your life will not last forever. Be nice to yourself, be nice to your partner, and draw on your reserves to get you through this time.

Remember to look after yourself. Eat well, get lots of sleep and avoid any pressure that can be avoided. Light a candle to remind you that dawn is coming.

There is no guarantee that this relationship will or should survive or that the relationship you are hoping to develop will develop. You may get what you hope for or you may face an ending. But a new beginning will follow.

Remember that this is not a call to action. This is asking you to acknowledge the darkness, rather than denying or resisting it. This will then bring you toward the light.

Love

When you open this book here, it is a wonderful opportunity to discover the real nature of love and to welcome it into your life.

Love is talked about, written about and sung about endlessly. We hear about romantic love, love at first sight, flowers and proposals. We hear about the excitement, the thrill and the joy of love, or the pain, hurt and sadness when it goes wrong. And we come to expect that if we are feeling these emotions we are experiencing love.

But none of these images and descriptions explains the true meaning of love, and because of this we look for love without any idea of what it is and what it will really mean for us either to give or to receive it. Are you searching for an idealized version of love? Do you feel you love someone without really knowing who they are? Do you say you love someone you don't like or trust? Then it is time to look at what you really know and understand about love. Remember that love develops over time. It's not appropriate to open your inner self to someone you have just met, no matter how attracted to them you are. For real love to develop, both partners must be willing to enter into the relationship and grow and learn together. Love isn't chasing after someone who is running away from you; it isn't letting yourself be smothered, hurt or put down and it isn't going along with what someone else wants. Love is best taken slowly, so give yourself time to get to know the other person and to judge whether they are worthy of the love you have to give. Are you both ready to commit to the challenge of nurturing and sharing a growing love?

Loving another person means going behind the public shop window you present, where you display what you feel is acceptable about yourself and instead you share the fears, doubts, dreams and hopes you keep locked away. It involves being brave, honest and open and letting another person get to know the parts of you which you feel are the least lovable and acceptable. It means opening up your most vulnerable inner self and learning to trust someone enough to let them come close and then even closer.

Being in a loving relationship with another person involves taking responsibility for yourself and accepting your responsibility toward the one you love. It means accepting that their feelings, beliefs and wishes are different from yours but just as valid, and letting go of trying to change them.

Above all love is knowing and being known for who you truly are with complete acceptance. To know another and to let yourself be known in this way is the most rewarding, joyous and nourishing experience life has to offer.

Power

When you open this book here, you can be very excited. Imagine that someone just gave you the energy of a power station to achieve whatever it is that you are trying to achieve.

There are a wealth of possibilities for your relationship or your potential relationship and the power for you to direct your life lies with you. This doesn't dismiss or disrespect the power of your partner or a potential partner, it simply emphasizes that you are more powerful right now than you realize.

Be clear and direct without being overwhelming. State what you want clearly and concisely and then start organizing how to get it, without disrespecting others or trying to control.

Remember that you have no power over anyone but yourself. If you give your power away and let your partner dictate everything, you will make yourself powerless.

Don't waste your power focusing on someone else. This is about you. What do you want that you can organize or manifest for yourself, with regard to relationships? You may need to break it all into smaller parts to accomplish your dream, but that is only technique. Know that the power is large.

Find ways to feel your power and feed your power without becoming oppressive. Say "no" when you mean "no." Make changes in your health, diet, finances, and home which reflect the fact that you have the power to shape your own life. Read other people's biographies for inspiration. This relationship isn't happening or about to happen to you. You are making it happen. Now is the time to acknowledge this and to shape it to work for you.

You are powerful.

Receive

When you open this book here, it is offering you both an instruction and a warning. It is easier to give than to receive and you are doing too much giving and not enough receiving. You need to change this.

When we are willing and open to receiving it is the time when life offers us the gifts that are there for the taking. So often we think that we have no issue with receiving, that we want to receive. But, in truth, we cannot.

To receive we have to be willing to stop giving for a while and to learn to simply receive what is offered. We don't have to earn it or trade for it. We have to be willing to create a space for another person to be able to come forward and fill it for us. It takes guts. It requires trust and it puts the focus on us, which can often feel uncomfortable. Yet it is a gift to others when we let them give to us.

What are you blocking? What won't you take? What won't you ask for? You need to ask yourself why you're doing this and what you are scared of. Are you willing to let someone know what it really is that you want? It doesn't matter how much we receive if it isn't what we value. Let yourself have what you really want.

Maybe you need to spend time working out what you want to receive from a relationship and life in general. Sometimes the first step is to trust that it really is safe for you to be honest about what you want. Do this now and then set about letting people know what this is. Then enjoy receiving it. Remember, you deserve it.

Control

When you open this book here it is time to look at the issue of control in your love life. Controlling behavior involves us making an effort to rule and direct how others think and feel as well as what they do. Although we have a hundred justifications for why we are being so controlling, we actually do it to make ourselves feel safe.

As children we had no control over what happened to us. If things were painful, difficult or frightening we were at the mercy of the adults around us. As we grew to be adults, we responded to this by finding ways of controlling ourselves and others. But being in a loving relationship means that we can't control things in the way that we can when we are alone. It reminds us of our childhood pain and we react to it by desperately trying to control our partners and they us. Pay attention to how you interfere in your partner's life and they in yours. How they dress, eat, or run their lives is none of your business and vice versa. You are only responsible for yourself and for dealing with the way that their behavior and choices affect you. Most important of all, believe that you can feel safe without trying to control everything around you. A sense of safety comes from inside, not outside yourself.

Now is the time to look at the way you relate to others. Do you bully or sulk to get what you want? Do you get sick, complain or act helpless without realizing or admitting how manipulative this is? Do you always think that your way is the best or the only way? These are all ways of attempting to control.

Accept that you have no power over others and that you can only control yourself. Step back and let others be who and what they are. Their choices are their own. If they pull away, let them go, even though it may cause you pain. If they treat you badly you can't make them change. Real love will only come to you from someone who is with you because they want to be, who treats you well because they want to.

If you are single and looking for love but not succeeding you need to realize that you are in control of this. It's easy to blame fate or bad luck but in fact you are picking people exactly because it won't work or because they're unavailable. Or, you are rejecting perfectly suitable partners on trumped-up reasoning. Doing this keeps you out of relationships, which is simply a way to stay in control. So start to behave toward others with generosity and to respect who they are. In this way you will draw love to you, not through control, but through giving love yourself.

Healing

When you open this book here, take comfort from the fact that whatever you are going through will leave you in a better, stronger place than before.

Healing can be calm and peaceful, or it can be turbulent and intense. Often when healing is taking place things can get worse before they get better. If this is happening, see it as a cleansing. You have to clear things out in order to move on. Sometimes we have to keep revisiting a painful experience until we finally get to its core, learn the lesson in it and then, and only then, are we able to leave it behind for good.

When we are in the process of healing around relationships, we often find that our health suffers. Are you having recurrent back problems, skin problems or a series of minor ailments? These are ways in which the body expresses its pain. Use them to draw your attention to your underlying emotional state. What do you need to heal? What do you need to grieve? It is important to support yourself at this time. Avoid extra pressure and go easy on yourself. Lower your expectations and, most importantly, stop criticizing yourself.

We find the experiences we need to heal our wounds from the past. You may not want to be dealing with this right now, but life gives us what we need before it gives us what we want. Know that your relationships can only benefit from this healing.

You may be healing yourself now in this relationship or healing old hurts to bring you on to the right relationship. You may be healing the relationship itself. Be positive and optimistic while acknowl-edging your pain. Healing can really hurt. But you can handle it. Try to work with this rather than pushing against it. Give it the time it requires. You're worth it. Remember that if you don't heal it now, you'll only be back in the same place, sometime soon.

The only way out is through, and healing is a sign that you are coming through.

Negativity

When you open this book here, it is a warning. You are being negative toward your relationship or the potential for a relationship. It may be that you have been disappointed recently, or that something is giving you a lot of difficulty. Negativity feeds on itself and then grows. It is time to turn away from being negative. If you don't want what you have, then let it go. But don't continue with this negativity. If you do want to keep your relationship or the possibility of a relationship, then stop being so negative and start being positive.

Focus on what is right. Focus on what you like, on what makes you happy. Focus on your partner's strengths and your own. When we turn from the negative to the positive we have hope and we develop greater appreciation for what we do have. This combination is the first step toward a brighter future.

Being negative is easy. It's lazy and it's cowardly. Which isn't to say that we should ignore things when they are wrong. By all means admit the problem but take a positive approach to it. When we are negative we can simply sit around and complain. To give this up requires effort. You deserve the effort and so does your future.

This also draws your attention to the negative energy around you. What is dragging you down? Do you need to alter your home or work environment or reconsider those that you have close contact with? You can always improve the energy around you by "clearing" in any way possible. Clear out clutter, reorganize your environment, clean things up, throw open the windows, change your habits, freshen anything that seems to need freshening, and don't lapse into laziness. Fresh energy is waiting for you and is much more rewarding.

Boundaries

When you open this book here, boundaries are your issue. A boundary is a limit which is defined at its farthest point. You can reach it but you are not to go beyond it.

We see physical boundaries all around us: the wall that divides our property from our neighbors'; the No Entry sign on a one-way street. Then there are the less physical boundaries such as the law that we live by and the promises we make and keep. Because the boundary marks the farthest point, crossing a boundary always has a consequence. We break the law, we get arrested. We break our promises, people stop trusting us. It works in reverse too. When others break our boundaries they get a reaction from us.

We all need boundaries in our love lives. We need to define where we begin and end. We need to set limits and make them known to ourselves and others. We need to be clear about what we find acceptable and unacceptable, what we will live with and what we will not tolerate. And we need to mean it.

When you open the book here you need to stop and look at your boundaries. Have you set yourself a boundary where you will only get involved with someone available? Are you sticking to it? Or are you letting someone treat you badly, putting up with dishonesty, cruelty or just subtle manipulation? Try looking at it from the outside. What would you think if a friend was being treated in this way?

In order for a boundary to be real you must be clear about the consequences of breaking it. If you say you're going to leave, you need to mean it—or you need to face the consequence, which may be to stay in the relationship and be bitter and withdrawn indefinitely. The consequence is what really happens, not what you say will happen. Without a consequence there is no boundary.

Setting boundaries and really sticking to them is challenging. It means getting clear about your bottom line. It means not getting caught up in what others think you should want or accept. You need to treat others with respect but you don't need to accept what is unacceptable as part of this. Ironically those around us are much more comfortable when we make and keep clear boundaries because then they know where they are with us.

Value yourself and know that you are entitled to your boundaries.

Patience

When you open this book here, the message is very simple. You need to have patience. Patience is an art form. It is the ability to stay in the present. To wait for what you want in a state of acceptance, trust and belief. Accepting that there is a time schedule that you are not in control of, often with no certainty of the outcome. Patience reminds us of our humanity. Just be with everything exactly as it is now. You don't have to do anything.

Patience has a lot of similarities to trust, except here we are focusing on timing and process, rather than on reassurance about the outcome. How patient are you? How easy do you find it to allow feelings and events to unfold at their own natural pace? How good are you at being in the present? For the moment, just focus on right now, not the future.

When we force events we can easily damage the end result. A good loaf needs time for the dough to rise, a butterfly needs to go through the process of being a caterpillar and in a chrysalis. Without patience for other people's timing and process, as well as our own, we push forward toward our goal but we miss the pleasure and benefits of the journey. We don't allow the foundations to set before we expect them to carry the weight of the building.

Slow down. Accept that things are how they are, each of you is who you are. You're meant to be exactly where you are right now. Whether it's financially, geographically, emotionally or attitudinally.

If you have a goal, then make a plan and act upon it, but ensure that you allow the appropriate time necessary. If it unfolds at a different pace or things are not where you want them to be—have patience.

Discover and learn the lesson of being in the present. Patience pays.

Unfinished Business

When you open this book here, it means that you need to finish whatever it is that remains unfinished, in order to establish a new relationship or for your current relationship to prosper.

Unfinished business is old business. It may be years old or from yesterday or last week. We didn't deal with something in a satisfactory manner at the time, often without realizing it. Then we brush it under the carpet, or to the back of our minds, and carry on as if it doesn't exist. The trouble with this is that then we never fully move on. Unfinished business takes up our attention and energy in a way that we're not aware of. It interferes with life now in unseen ways. It's similar to putting the receiver down by the side of the phone instead of breaking the connection properly, freeing the line for new calls.

If we don't finish something properly it prevents us from starting something else afresh. It's like leaving your rubbish to pile up in the kitchen and then stepping around it, pretending it's not there. The longer you leave it, the better you get at pretending it's not there but the smellier it becomes. And the more of it that you pile up, the harder it is to move freely around your kitchen. Eventually it contaminates everything without you realizing it.

Unfinished business damages relationships. What haven't you dealt with? What needs to be said that you're avoiding saying? What old resentments, hurts, wishes or dreams are you sitting on, which you need to pull out, dust off and deal with? In your relationship is there something that you have both brushed under the carpet but that actually really matters? Face it and you'll both benefit from your bravery.

This also includes unfinished business from previous relationships. Otherwise it will interfere with your current one or with the making of a new one. Who do you need to apologize to? Who are you still mad at? Who are you still in love with, or hate with? What haven't you really grieved or let go of? Now is the time to deal with it.

You don't necessarily have to involve the other person for you to finish something off properly. You can do this alone. For example, write a letter including everything you want to say and then when you have finished, burn it ceremonially. Do it again and again until it feels finished. You have to do what it takes and face what needs to be faced, because only then will you be free.

96

Breakup

When you open this book here, it signifies endings. It may be that the relationship is literally ending. This can mean divorce or separation. If your relationship is ending, it asks you to trust the process and know that there is light at the end of the tunnel. This is happening for the best, even if it doesn't feel like it right now. Accept the pain and it will slowly diminish. You can handle this.

This can also mark a breakthrough in the relationship where it dies in its current form and is reborn anew. Usually this will involve some form of separation, however temporary. Endings mark the need to move on, to let the relationship die, whether it is to be reborn in a new form or not. Due to the continual cycles of life and death, some form of rebirth will always follow an ending, so trust this process and go with it. You will find the partner who is right for you, whether it is this person or someone new.

It may be that a breakup with a third party is necessary for the success of a relationship. Who are you overinvolved with, outside the romantic context? Is it time you left home or let go of your best friend or old boyfriend? You need to allow space for your true, primary, romantic relationship to develop. If you are hoping to establish a new relationship, know that there is someone that you need to separate from before you will find your new partner. Let go of any attachment to an old relationship or ex-partner. End your desire or fantasy for a new relationship to develop with someone specific who you have your eye on. Cut your ties and free yourself so that life can lead you to the right relationship, rather than to the one that you think you want.

One door opens when another one closes. Now you have to close the door, or accept its closing, and trust that another one will open. It really will. Moving on is a part of life. Be brave.

It is only when we dare to leave that we are free to stay on our own terms or free to find something new.

Spiritual Connection

When you open this book here, the spirits around you want to remind you that you are more than just flesh and blood. You have an inner essence which needs attending to.

It asks you to go a little deeper. To develop, renew or strengthen your connection to your role in this world.

We are all intimately connected on a cosmic level. Look up at the sky. Know that the universe and the galaxies stretch far out and around us. Look into a flower or your fingernail and know that this scale works in the other direction too. Within each detail there is greater detail.

We are existing in a chain of awareness and energy. All perfectly held in our place, in our particular existence. Right now everything is exactly as it should be. And then we move on and things change and that is right too. Know that you are protected and that you are not alone. Angels hover constantly around you waiting to help. Yet they must be requested to help us before they can interfere. Those who come before us watch over us and guide us, so let that guidance in. Find the best balance between the physical and spiritual world that works for you.

Often we neglect our connection with a more powerful force than ourselves, as we all try to play God in our own lives. Let your spirituality guide your relationships. Follow your instincts to do what needs to be done at each moment in time.

Light a candle and look into the flame. The light signifies the energy in each of us and the world around us. Offer up your thanks for anything that you appreciate and invite the spirits into your love life. They're waiting for your call.

Let Go

When you open this book here, you are presented with one of the biggest challenges in relationships and in life itself. But the reward you reap will be in proportion to the effort expended. It's simple— let go. What if it wasn't up to you? What if you couldn't control others, yourself, the outcome, today, tomorrow, forever?

This isn't calling for you to be passive or to stop caring. It's telling you to take a backseat. It's not telling you to leave the relationship, or to stop trying to establish a new one, but it is telling you to let it be what it really is. Get your nose (and anything else you've got in there) out of everyone else's business. Let them look after their own lives and you look after yours. Stop trying to make the world fit with your desires. Let it be what it is and then deal with it as it is.

Let fate and destiny bring you what they will. Sit down, breathe, take some time out or time off and let life just happen for once. If you are trying to convince, educate, pressurize or manipulate your partner, or someone new, into giving you what you want, now is the time to stop. If you are pushing yourself in the same way—stop. Who would you be if you just let go? Who knows what experiences and opportunities you're missing out on, while being so busy and holding on so tightly, trying to manipulate everything and everyone so intensely.

Watch what happens when you begin to let go. It will all work out exactly as it's meant to and better than it will with you trying to control it. Have faith that life will support you and bring you what you need. Let the fear that you won't get what you want surface, and deal with that instead of avoiding it. You'll never be able to swim to a new shore if you won't let go of the driftwood you're holding on to so tightly.

Swim, let go, let the tide direct you, let the water of life support your weight. It's safe to let go. Do it now.

Change of Fortune

When you open this book here, it is a profound moment. You can relax and celebrate. This signifies that things are about to improve significantly. If you have been struggling with difficulties then the struggle will soon be over. Good times are ahead. Peace and harmony are close at hand and the breakthrough that you've been hoping for will present itself.

If life is good and your relationship is good, be happy in the knowledge that it's going to get even better. Change of Fortune marks a significant step forward, so dream your dreams and know that they will soon arrive.

If you are hoping to find a new relationship, trust that you will. If things have been difficult, know that it's all going to get much easier. This signifies improvement wherever you are in the romantic scheme of things. Change of Fortune promises you that the future is truly bright.

This is a good time to prepare yourself for what lies ahead. What do you put off through wasting time worrying about the future? Feel free to get on with it now. What changes would you make if you knew that you couldn't lose? Get active. This encourages you to change your own fortune as well as reassuring you that good fortune lies ahead. Take advantage of this moment. Admit what it is that you really want to say or do. Follow your heart, be brave, be adventurous and know that you are supported. The time is right.

Don't forget your responsibilities, show respect for others and stay honest. As long as you follow these three rules, the time is right to jump. You are fortunate.

Anger

When you open this book here, it brings your attention to the anger present in your relationship or interfering with the establishment of new relationships. This will not surprise you if you are already aware of your anger. But if you are not aware of being angry, this tells you that you are. You need to deal with it. Knowing about it isn't enough and complaining about it won't help.

First of all, get clear what it is that you're angry about. Write it out on a piece of paper, talk it through with someone, or do whatever works for you, until you're sure you know what you're really angry about.

It may seem like you're reacting to one thing when actually you're angry about something completely unconnected. Check this out with yourself. We often pick the easy topics to focus our anger on because we feel that we can't justify our anger over the issue that's most important to us. Often, focusing on the real issue makes us feel too vulnerable.

Remember, all anger is always both justified and valid. Other people don't have to agree with us but we can get angry over anything. Anger is a feeling. You can't choose not to have it. It's either there or it isn't. If you deny it because you think it's unacceptable, you're only hiding it, not stopping it. It will go underground and fester and damage a relationship anyway. So admit you're angry and then find a way to express it safely. Write a letter you don't need to send or shout at a cushion or chair, pretending it's another person. If someone else is involved leave them out of it completely until you've expressed it away from them. Otherwise you'll regret it. Only then will you be ready to let it go or to discuss it with them reasonably.

If you're sure you're not angry and think that this must relate to your partner, or potential partner, you're mistaken. They may be angry too, but this is about you.

Acceptance

When you open this book here, the message is very important. It is about letting those that we have relationships with, or hope to have relationships with, be themselves—accepting who they really are.

It's a tall order. Mostly when we have relationships we want to change the other person to who we want them to be, regardless of who they really are. Acceptance is asking you to stop this. Trying to change someone we're having a relationship with doesn't work for them and it doesn't work for you. If you want them to be different, then have the relationship with someone else who is already what you want. If you really want the relationship with this specific person, then you need to accept them as they are. If they wish to change themselves it is their business and their responsibility. You have no power over anyone else. So the sooner you accept who they are and how they are, the better.

What you do have power over is your reaction to who the other person is. You can find it acceptable or unacceptable and you can tell them this. But remember, what they do with that information is up to them. You need to accept this too. Stop denying who they are or pretending they're someone they're not.

If you ask someone kindly and specifically to change a particular behavior, they may have the goodwill to do so. Appreciate this and support them. But if they won't, they won't. Step back and have a good look at who this person really is and accept it. Remember, much of what may need to change will actually be you and your behavior. It's always easier to put the focus on someone else.

We are all perfect, exactly as we are, with all of our faults and endearing qualities. Stop trying to force someone untidy to become tidy, or someone dishonest to be honest, or someone lively to be quiet. Enjoy who they are or move away from them and move on, but stop trying to change them. Then maybe you can begin to accept who you really are too and have the confidence to declare it. Then you can be appreciated by those who accept you for you and let go of those who don't.

Jealousy

When you open this book here, jealousy is operating. It is important to admit to jealousy and learn from it, rather than deny it. Otherwise it will be very damaging to your relationship or desire for a relationship.

If you feel jealous of your partner, check whether they are behaving appropriately. Are they prioritizing their commitment and loyalty to you? Check whether jealousy is actually a warning signal that you are not the priority when you should be. Don't put up with someone who doesn't treat you with the respect that you deserve. Or perhaps their behavior is fine and your jealousy stems from your insecurity and low self-esteem. Address these and you'll find that your jealousy disappears.

Jealousy operates in many areas of our relationships. You may be jealous of someone else in relation to your partner or you may be jealous of their confidence, success, lifestyle or their relationships with friends, family or work. When we are jealous, we are envious in a negative way, which means that we want something that someone else has. Our refusal to acknowledge that desire creates the bitterness and pain of jealousy. But if we have the courage to be honest about our feelings we can use jealousy in a positive way. What is it that you are jealous of? Does someone else have qualities or elements in their lifestyle or relationship that you wish for? Start working out how to get these things for yourself rather than resenting those who have them already. Use these desires to motivate you, rather than turning your energy against another person. Go after whatever it is that you are jealous of for yourself. But remember to do it in your own style. You can't become someone else; you must learn to develop who you are.

Also, look at the price that the other person pays for having what it is that you are jealous of. Are you willing to organize yourself or your life in the way which would be necessary for you to have what they have? Is it worth the effort to you? Is it worth the sacrifice? If it isn't, then appreciate them for their choice but admit that in reality you don't actually want the whole package. Jealousy is an easy way to resent what others have without being willing to take the consequences, good or bad, of having it ourselves. Admit that your choices work for you, unless of course they don't—in which case make some changes. Work on your self-esteem and your self-confidence. No one else is lucky enough to be you. Appreciate that.

Pain

When you open this book here, it means that right now you are hurting. You may be very aware of this or denying it, but you are in pain. Are you suffering from a broken heart, having been let down by someone that you love? Or have you recently ended a relationship because it wasn't right? When things have gone badly the pain doesn't end when the relationship ends. You need to give yourself the time to grieve. Don't just rush into something new or you'll take your pain into the next relationship where it will cause unnecessary damage.

If you are single at the moment, your pain may be from loneliness, because you long for someone special to share a relationship with. The world may seem full of couples and it can be especially painful being around others who have the companionship that you so wish for.

Being in established relationships can also be very painful. Sometimes it's hard to accept how much it can hurt. Throughout our lives we are sold the fantasy that love will be a totally wonderful experience. No one tells us the truth, that love involves pain as well as pleasure. It's all too easy to move on whenever being in a relationship begins to hurt, but if you do this you will always be moving on. Stay committed and deal with the pain. Share with your partner what hurts and together work on learning how to support each other when you are in pain.

What you most need to understand is that this pain that you are ascribing to love or the need for love has little or nothing to do with romance and relationships. It stems from the deeply buried hurts of childhood. You expect love to take you away from your feeling of emptiness or from the ache deep inside you. You are using romance and companionship as a drinker uses alcohol, to avoid your feelings or being left alone with yourself. What is happening in your love life is only happening to help you bring your childhood pain to awareness so that you can deal with it. And when you do, you will find that you are more successful in love and all aspects of love will be less painful.

Right now you need to accept your pain and welcome it into your life. You may imagine that you can't bear to do this, but avoiding your pain is what really hurts; experiencing it brings a real and lasting sense of relief.

You can handle it. Pain is part of loving. Be brave and remember to be kind to yourself.